SPORTS FOR SPROUTS

Baseball

Holly Karapetkova

ROURKE PUBLISHING

Vero Beach, Florida 32964

www.rourkepublishing.com

Photo credits: Cover © Wendy Nero; Title Page © Wendy Nero, Crystal Kirk, Leah-Anne Thompson, vnosokin, Gerville Hall, Rob Marmion; Page 3 © Ben Blankenburg; Page 4 © Rob Friedman; Page 7 © Rob Friedman; Page 8 © Wendy Nero; Page 11 © Rob Friedman; Page 12 © RichVintage; Page 14 © Rob Friedman; Page 17 © sonyae; Page 18 © Rob Friedman; Page 21 © Fejas; Page 22 © Terry Poche, Rob Friedman, Neil Roy Johnson; Page 23 © Amy Smith, Samuel Acosta, RichVintage; Sidebar Silhouettes © Sarah Nicholl

Editor: Meg Greve

Cover and page design by Nicola Stratford, Blue Door Publishing

Library of Congress Cataloging-in-Publication Data

Karapetkova, Holly.
  Baseball / Holly Karapetkova.
    p. cm. -- (Sports for sprouts)
  ISBN 978-1-60694-321-2 (hard cover)
  ISBN 978-1-60694-821-7 (soft cover)
  ISBN 978-1-60694-562-9 (bilingual)
  1. Baseball--Juvenile literature. I. Title.
  GV867.5.K37 2009
  796.357--dc22
                                    2009002253

Printed in the USA

CG/CG

www.rourkepublishing.com - rourke@rourkepublishing.com
Post Office Box 643328 Vero Beach, Florida 32964

I play baseball.

3

4

I wear baseball pants and a baseball **glove**.

I am on a team. Our team plays **offense** and **defense**.

7

8

Our team has many players. When we play defense, I play catcher.

When we play offense, I get to bat. I wear a **helmet**.

11

I hold the bat and swing. I hit the ball.

14

I run to first, second, and third **base**. Then I run to **home plate**.

Home run!

16

We don't always win.
But I still love baseball!

Where do you want to play?

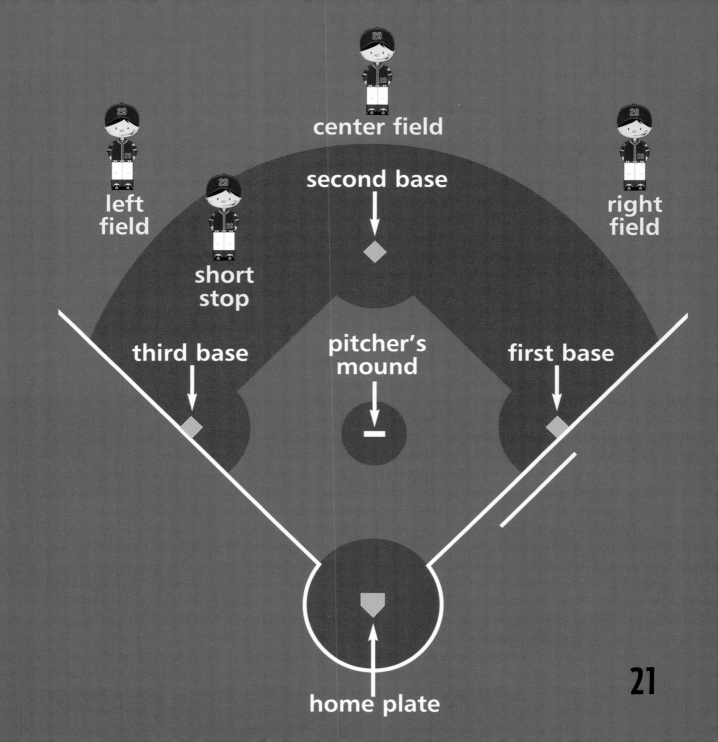

center field

second base

left field

right field

short stop

third base

pitcher's mound

first base

home plate

21

Glossary

base (BAYSS): A base is a spot on the field where a player runs after the ball is hit. There are three bases on the baseball field: first base, second base, and third base.

defense (DEE-fenss): When a team is on defense, the players try to keep the other team from scoring.

glove (GLUHV): A glove is a special covering that baseball players wear on the hand they catch with. It is much bigger than a hand and is usually made out of leather.

helmet (HEL-mit): A helmet is a special hard hat that baseball players wear. The helmet protects them from getting hit in the head when they are at bat.

home plate (HOME PLAYT): Home plate is where the batter stands and tries to hit the ball. It is also where the players run to score one point after they have touched first, second, and third bases.

offense (AW-fenss): When a team is on offense, the players try to score.

Index

base   15, 21
baseball glove   5
baseball pants   5
bat   10, 13
catcher   9

helmet   10
hit   13
home plate   15, 21
home run   16
team   6, 9

Websites

www.exploratorium.edu/baseball/bouncing_balls.html
www.littleleague.org
www.pony.org

About The Author

Holly Karapetkova, Ph.D., loves writing books and poems for kids and adults. She teaches at Marymount University and lives in the Washington, D.C., area with her husband, her son K.J., and her two dogs, Muffy and Attila.